Lukas FOSS

ELEGY
for Clarinet and Piano

Edited by Richard Stoltzman

Clarinet in Bb

Rental materials for Clarinet and Orchestra
available exclusively from Keiser Classical:

1-855-259-6495 Toll-free (U.S./ Canada)
rental@laurenkeisermusic.com

KEISER
CLASSICAL

Clarinet in B♭

Edited by Richard Stoltzman

to Artie Shaw

ELEGY

for Clarinet in B♭ and Orchestra

LUKAS FOSS
(1949)

Clarinet in B♭